WALKS AROUND Helmsley

10 WALKS 6 MILES OR LESS

Dalesman

Dalesman Publishing Company Ltd
Stable Courtyard, Broughton Hall,
Skipton, North Yorkshire BD23 3AZ

First Edition 1999

Text © Nick Channer

Illustrations © Christine Isherwood:
p5 ragged robin, ladies smock and marsh marigold, p11 red grouse,
p18 merlin, p21 northern argus, p26 spotted flycatcher, p32 poppies

Maps by Jeremy Ashcroft

Cover : Helmsley by Roger Kilvington

A British Library Cataloguing in Publication record
is available for this book

ISBN 1 85568 164 1

Printed by Amadeus Press, Huddersfield

Contents

Introduction

The picturesque market town of Helmsley acts as a natural gateway to the many and varied delights of the North York Moors. Its charming setting at the entrance to Ryedale makes it a popular choice for visitors, and, for as long as local residents can remember, people from all corners of Britain have used the town as a convenient base from which to tour the national park.

Apart from its famous ruined castle, one of Helmsley's greatest assets is its close proximity to some of the most spectacular walking country in the land. The book begins with two walks to the south-west of Helmsley, exploring the rolling, wooded country along the southern rim of the North York Moors. A few miles to the west of the town lies the escarpment of the Cleveland and Hambleton Hills, representing the North York Moors National Park's western boundary. This lofty range of windswept hills offers many miles of superb walking, and from Sutton Bank, where the third walk begins, the vastness of the fertile Vale of York stretches away under huge skies to the west.

Further north lies the remote village of Hawnby where a spectacular walk allows you to appreciate at first hand the unique beauty and grandeur of the region. Heading back towards Helmsley brings you to the ruins of Rievaulx Abbey, one of North Yorkshire's loveliest landmarks and the starting point for the next walk. The abbey inspired the likes of Wordsworth and Turner and its peaceful, wooded setting is truly delightful.

Two routes start from the Market Square in Helmsley; one takes you swiftly from the bustling town centre into a sheltered wooded dale, while the other walk heads south following part of the long-distance Ebor Way beside the placid waters of the River Rye. The penultimate walk takes advantage of the gentle lowland country to the south of Helmsley, and when you have finished the final circuit, which starts at Nunnington and offers regal views over a spacious rural landscape, a visit to Nunnington Hall, a part-16th century manor house on the banks of the Rye, is recommended — opening times permitting.

Helmsley is also the official starting point for the horseshoe-shaped Cleveland Way, Britain's second oldest national long-distance path, opened in 1969. Keeping close to the North York Moors National Park's boundary for much of the way, the 110-mile route divides into two distinct halves. Initially, it follows the dramatic escarpment of the Hambleton and Cleveland Hills before cutting across country to Saltburn where it heads south along the Heritage Coast, finishing at Filey Brigg. Several walks described in this book include sections of the Cleveland Way.

Ampleforth and Studford Ring

Length of Walk: 4 miles
Start/finish: Ampleforth village centre, south of the A170 between Sutton Bank and Helmsley
Terrain: Wooded slopes, field paths, and an easy stretch of country road over high-level ground. One lengthy climb through woodland

This splendidly-wooded walk soon plunges deep into thickly afforested country to the north-west of Ampleforth. Many of the views are breathtaking, with the wooded slopes of Yearsley Moor to the south constantly in sight.

Mention Ampleforth and most people think of the village's famous Roman Catholic public school. But Ampleforth is very much a community in its own right, with a prosperous air and a long main street overlooked by rows of striking stone-built houses and cottages. The school, which was originally an abbey founded by Benedictine monks who fled from France to avoid persecution during the French Revolution, opened for business in 1802 with just two pupils.

One of Ampleforth's 20th-century headmasters commissioned Robert Thompson, the famous woodcarver of nearby Kilburn, to design furniture for the school. Thompson also made a wooden cross for the parish church, which contains an intriguing 14th-century effigy, depicting a bearded man praying with a woman peering over his shoulder.

5

Follow the village street in a westerly direction, up the slope and past the speed derestriction sign. Pass a turning on the right for Hambleton. Continue for about 30yds/m and then turn right into Westwood Lane. Keep going when the surface of the lane becomes rougher underfoot. The lane climbs gently and dips several times and between the trees are tantalizing glimpses of distant wooded countryside and afforested slopes. Pass a footpath sign and emerge from the trees, following the track as it curves to the right.

On reaching a hairpin bend, veer right to join a path skirting a fence. There is a stream down below on the left. Beyond the next stile, water can be seen gushing from an underground spring. Follow the waymarked path between trees and margins of undergrowth. Climb quite steeply, rising above a wooded hollow on the right. Foxgloves and different species of fern can be seen lining the path. Many wild flowers and plants, including harebells, grow here too.

At a junction with a wide forest track, turn left and follow it as it bends to the right. The soothing sigh of the breeze in the trees is probably the only sound to break the silence on this stretch of the walk. Merge with another track further on and continue through the forest, climbing gently between the trees. The ascent becomes progressively steeper and on reaching a left bend, look for a path on the right, running through the undergrowth to the road. Bear right, avoid a turning on the right and continue along High Street. Pass the entrance to Studford Farm and keep going until the road reaches a footpath sign and stile on the right.

Cross into the field, keep the woodland on the left and pass the banks of Studford Ring, a Bronze Age stock enclosure. Continue in a south-westerly direction and look for a stile and gate where the field tapers. Follow a grassy track, with striking views over to the wooded slopes of Yearsley Moor. To the west of the moor lies Newburgh Priory, built by the Augustinians in 1145. Some sources suggest that the body of Oliver Cromwell lies buried there, though this theory has generated a great deal of controversy over the years.

On reaching a gate, follow the track to the left and after 60yds/m, just before the next gate, turn right at a stile. Head down the left boundary of the field to a gate and in the next field aim diagonally right to a stile. Cross a paddock to a stile in its southerly boundary, then join a stony track from which there are glimpses of Ampleforth below.

Cross a stile on the right after about 90yds/m and descend the bank, which can be slippery in wet weather. Go over a track to join a path running

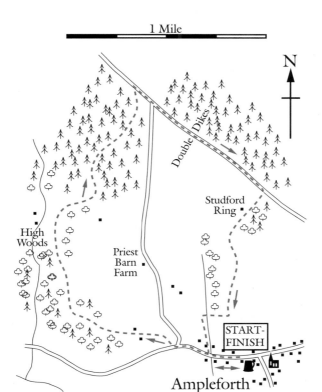

through the undergrowth. Follow the path into some woodland and when it veers right, go straight ahead to a stile. Cross a beck and then hug the field boundary as far as a stile on the left. Join a woodland path and follow it through the trees until it reaches the garden of a private house. Make for the left of the garage, still on a public right of way, and follow the narrow path, then the drive, to the road. Turn left and return to the centre of Ampleforth.

Wass and Byland Abbey

Length of walk: 3¹/₂ miles
Start/finish: Wass village centre, south of the A170, midway between Helmsley and Sutton Bank
Terrain: Undulating field paths and brief stretches of country road

Circular walk exploring swathes of rolling countryside below the Hambleton Hills and visiting the spectacular remains of Byland Abbey.

Next door to the more famous village of Ampleforth, Wass shelters in a broad cleft 600ft below the wooded, south escarpment of the Hambleton Hills, looking directly across a shallow valley which connects the western edge of the Vale of Pickering with the Vale of Mowbray. Much of the village was built with stones taken from Byland Abbey following the Dissolution of the Monasteries.

From the centre of Wass, walk along the main road towards Byland Abbey. On the left is the Wombwell Arms, one of the area's most historic pubs. The building dates back to the 17th century and includes a former granary. Pass a telephone box on the right and walk down to the right-hand bend. Turn left here and cross two stiles to reach a field. Bear right and make for the stile in the boundary. The ground here can be wet and boggy, so a little delicate footwork is necessary!

The rooftops of Wass are clearly seen over to the left as you cross the field, the village dominated by the wooded hills rising above it. Pass under some power cables and make for the top right-hand corner of the field, crossing two stiles to the road. Turn right and follow the road between fence and hedgerows. Just before it bends rather sharply to the left, look for a footpath running off to the left and squeeze through the hedge to a stile.

Follow the path across the grassy, lower slopes of the hillside, keeping parallel to the road. A spectacular curtain of trees can be seen drawn across the skyline to the left. Make for a gate and continue following the path in the next field. Cross a footbridge located amongst some trees up ahead and cut across the next field to a gap in the hedge where there is a stile. Cross a track leading to Carr House and keep going in the next field. Much of the return leg of the walk to Wass can be seen from this vantage point, the path cutting across the fields to the south of the road.

Make for another stile and cross a lumpy field, with a dilapidated shed on the left. Extensive woodland can be seen rising above it. Head for a stile and footbridge in the field corner and pass beneath power cables in the next field. Make for the far corner and look for a stile leading out to the road. Turn left and follow it as far as a footpath sign and stile on the right. Descend the grassy path on the right, with spectacular views across the south-west corner of the North York Moors National Park dominating this stage of the walk. Cross a stile beside a gate in the next boundary and head diagonally down the field slope. Continue ahead at the next stile and cross a small field, making now for a footbridge.

Veer diagonally right and the gable end of a byre can be seen now on the hilltop. Cross a stile and continue in the next field, heading towards the building. Follow the path to the left of the byre and then curve left in front of a pond. Make for the corner of the fence enclosing the pond and look for two galvanized gates. Pass through the left gate and follow the track along

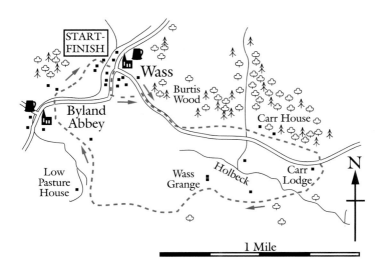

the field edge to the next gate. Over to the right lie the buildings of Wass Grange. Go straight on in the next field, passing under power cables, and keep the farm track parallel on the right. When the track bends sharp right, veer off to the left towards a belt of woodland. Follow the grassy track as it curves right, in front of the trees, and make for a gate. Turn right immediately beyond it and skirt the field.

Keep going until you see a waymark in the hedgerow on the right. Cut across the field, following the grassy path up to the next stile. Head up the field slope to a second waymark, walk ahead and keep to the left of some gorse bushes down near the left-hand field boundary. Using further waymarks to guide you, curve right and make for a gap in the field corner by some trees. The outline of Low Pasture House looms into view ahead at this stage. Follow the path to the right of the house, where a beck can be seen scurrying below. When it twists away to the left, go straight out across the field ahead. The ruins of Byland Abbey edge into view now, set against a splendid, wooded backdrop. Cross the next stile into a tree-ringed field and pass through a gap in the right-hand boundary hedge. Walk towards the abbey ruins and turn right when you reach a fence enclosing the site.

Byland Abbey dates back to 1177 and eventually became the largest Cistercian church in Britain. It was from here that Edward II was forced to flee in 1322 when the Scots stumbled upon his army at nearby Scotch Corner, routing it at the Battle of Byland. The Scots made off with just about everything the king left behind, ransacking the Abbey into the bargain. The distinctive glazed tiles laid out in geometric patterns and the surviving west front, which includes the remains of a rose window, are a vivid reminder of how magnificent Byland Abbey once was.

Keep the ruins close by on the left, cross a field to a stile and emerge at the roadside. Go straight across to join a tarmacked drive leading to Abbey House. Swing right after several steps to a stile. Cross the pasture to a second stile, veer diagonally left in the next field and pass under some power cables. Make for the top corner of the field where there is a gate. Curve left in the next field and head for a second gate. Follow a grassy track to the road, turn right and return to the centre of Wass.

Sutton Bank

Length of walk: 4 miles
Start/finish: Sutton Bank Information Centre car park on the A170
between Thirsk and Helmsley
Terrain: After a stretch of quiet country road, the walk follows field
paths and bridle tracks to link up with the route of the Cleveland Way

Keeping within sight of the National Park's western boundary, the route heads north along the rim of the Hambleton Hills, crossing high-level farmland before eventually turning south to reach the Cleveland Way. The windswept scarp overlooks a stunning panorama, conveying the impression that the whole of the North of England is spread out below.

The Sutton Bank Information Centre provides detailed information on the North York Moors National Park. Near the centre's entrance are the remains of an old grouse butt, its cracks and crevices making a perfect habitat for all manner of spiders and insects. Now that animals no longer graze here, conifers and native broadleaved trees are beginning to colonize the ground surrounding the building. Birch is among the most common species found in this area.

Head north-east from the centre and take the road signposted Old Byland, Cold Kirby and Hawnby. Follow the lane, soon passing the entrance to Garbutt Farm, and a glance to the right brings an expansive moorland landscape into focus. Bear left at the next road junction, then left again after a few steps to join a bridleway by the entrance to Dialstone Farm.

The farm, originally a drovers' inn, used to be the venue for the Hambleton Race Ground. The races became something of a tradition in the area and jockeys competed with one another for the treasured trophies, donated by eminent patrons of the day, including George I and Queen Anne. Dialstone probably takes its name from the dial, or weighing machine, used for weighing jockeys before each race.

Follow the track between fields, heading towards a copse. Turn right just before the trees and keep a field boundary on the right. The buildings of Dialstone Farm can be seen over to the right, set against a curtain of trees. Follow the fence and crumbling remains of a wall, bear right at the corner and continue alongside the boundary for about 100yds/m.

Turn left, almost level with the farm, and follow an unfenced, grassy path between fields. Make for a gap in the next boundary, denoted by a bridleway sign. Turn left and skirt a field. This stretch of the walk stimulates a sense of anticipation that is quickly rewarded. Each step brings one of the North of England's finest panoramas ever closer into view, and before long the Vale of York, a vast, rural patchwork of field patterns, trees and hedgerows, can be seen stretching as far as the Pennine chain to the west. James Herriot, who lived nearby until his death in 1995, described this view as the finest in England. Wordsworth watched the sun go down from this spot on his wedding day.

Pass a bridleway sign, drop down a slope to the route of the Cleveland Way and turn left. Don't be surprised to see gliders swooping silently overhead. The Yorkshire Gliding Club is nearby. Follow the well-used path along the rim of the escarpment, above the trees of South Woods. Pass a sign for the Cleveland Way and continue towards Sutton Bank. Avoid a bridleway to Dialstone Farm and pass a sign which reads 'no horses or cycles — footpath only'. Gormire Lake, fed by underwater springs, edges into view down below, its smooth surface reflecting the thick woodland surrounding it.

Above the lake is the awesome precipice of Whitestone Cliff. Heavy rockfall in the mid-18th century exposed a sheer white face which can be seen from many miles away. The path along the cliff edge is unfenced. Take great care. Further on, the Cleveland Way becomes enveloped by trees and foliage before revealing views of traffic negotiating the steep one-in-four climb to the summit of Sutton Bank. The road has long been famous for its perilous conditions in winter. Coaches once used this route but are now prohibited.

Pass a seat, suitably placed to take advantage of the view, and continue through a tunnel of trees. The buildings of the glider station can be seen ahead, above the tree-clad slopes. Cross the minor road and return to the car park.

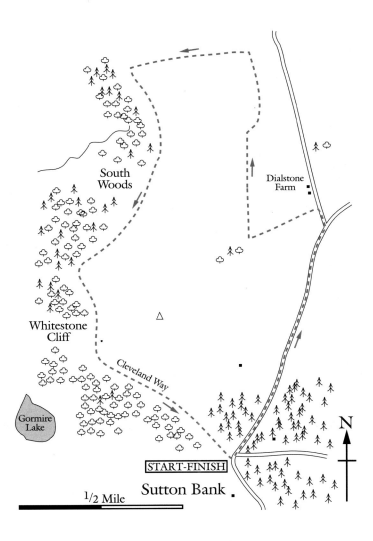

South
Woods

Dialstone
Farm

Whitestone
Cliff

Cleveland Way

Gormire
Lake

N

START-FINISH

Sutton Bank

1/2 Mile

Cold Kirby and the Cleveland Way

Length of walk: 4 miles
Start/finish: Cold Kirby village centre, about 2 miles from Sutton Bank
Terrain: Field and woodland paths and tracks; one stretch of quiet road.
Several ascents and descents and a gradual climb out of Flassen Dale

Circular walk which cuts across open upland country to the village of Scawton then returns to Cold Kirby via Flassen Dale and a stretch of the Cleveland Way.

With the church on your left head down the track and when it swings left, go straight ahead over a stile beside a gate. Walk up the slope to cross breezy farmland and when the track sweeps left, go straight on along a footpath towards woodland. Make for a stile in the bottom corner of the field and follow the path, which can be slippery, down into the trees of Flassen Dale. On reaching a path, turn right to a fork. Take the lower path here and descend through the trees to a woodland ride running along the dale floor. Turn left and walk along to a small pond on the right. Take the path immediately beyond it, climbing steeply up the bank through the trees.

Cross a stile on the edge of the wood and make for a second stile across the field in the opposite boundary. Go straight over and down the field edge, keeping hedge and fence on the right. Cross another stile and keep to the right of the fence in the next field. Follow the path through a gateway and join a field track curving to the right. Swing sharp left immediately beyond a line of trees and follow a grassy track running up alongside the woodland. Cross a stile and continue ahead with the trees on the left. Aim to the left of Pond Farm, pass through a gate and then veer right to a stile leading onto a woodland path. Follow it to the road at Scawton. To visit The Hare Inn, turn right and walk along the main street. The pub dates back to the 18th century, replacing an earlier hostelry where, in the 17th century, ale was brewed for iron workers employed by the Earl of Rutland.

Suitably refreshed, retrace your steps through the village. Scawton lies on the west bank of the River Rye and the road running through the village was originally used by travellers from the North. Among them were the monks of Rievaulx Abbey who built the medieval bridge over the Rye, destroyed by floods in 1754. The village church was originally a chapel, built by the monks of Byland Abbey in the 12th century. Follow the road out of Scawton and after about half a mile it bends right. Go straight on at this point, passing through a gate at the entrance to Stocking House Farm. Once through the gate, veer half left to join a woodland bridleway.

Descend the slope towards Nettle Dale, a side valley, and when you emerge from the tree cover, a footbridge is visible ahead. Cross the track and follow the signs for the Cleveland Way. Use the stepping stones to cross the beck and make for a gate. Avoid the stile in front of you and follow the track, with a footbridge and the tree-clad slopes of Callister Wood over to your right. Keep left at the next junction and continue on the Cleveland Way as it cuts through Flassen Dale.

Turn right at the next intersection, following the waymarks for this long-distance national trail, and begin a gradual climb through the trees to reach exposed farmland above the trees of the dale. Pass some corrugated barns and the rooftops of Cold Kirby edge into view ahead. When the track bends left, veer right down the slope, still following the Cleveland Way. Head up the grassy hillside into the village and the church can be seen over to the left.

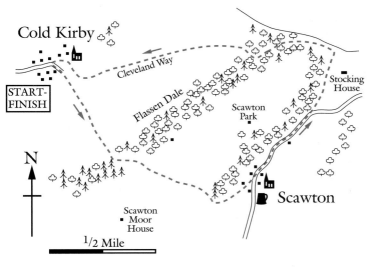

Hawnby

Length of walk: 2 miles
Start/finish: Hawnby village centre, north-west of Helmsley, off the B1257
Terrain: Sheltered valley paths and tracks, a stretch of quiet country road.
A lengthy but undemanding climb between the Ladhill Beck and the road

Short circular walk beginning in the village of Hawnby and heading north through the valley of the Ladhill Beck. The route provides views of some of the National Park's most spectacular scenery.

Idyllic Hawnby, which lies deep in hill country on a spur overlooking the River Rye, is one of the most isolated villages in this corner of the North York Moors National Park. John Wesley preached here in 1757, describing the surrounding countryside as 'one of the pleasantest parts of England'. The Abbot of Byland and the Prioress of Arden came to this spot 800 years ago to try and settle the differences between their respective houses. Have a look at Hawnby before starting the walk, admire the village's red-roofed cottages and pause to enjoy the little 12th-century church's pretty, sheltered setting. To the left of the altar of All Saints is a painted memorial tablet to Anne Tankard, who died in infancy in 1608. The tiny child is depicted asleep in her cradle beside a lily and a rosebush, with a clock whose time is set permanently between one and two, a poignant reminder of how short this little girl's life was.

Head east out of the village, dropping downhill at the junction towards Laskill. When the road bends sharp right by a sign for a ford, go straight on through a gate. Follow the path along the edge of dense woodland, emerge into a field and then go down the slope to a footbridge. There are impressive views here of steeply rising hillsides cloaked with trees. Cross the Ladhill Beck and follow the path running alongside it; further on it merges with a clear track heading north to a gate and extensive woodland. Keep right when the track forks, pass through a second gate and continue through the trees. Veer right when you see a sign advising walkers that the path ahead is not a right of way.

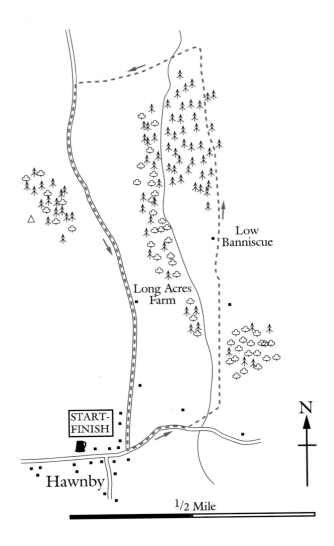

Low
Banniscue

Long Acres
Farm

START-
FINISH

Hawnby

N

1/2 Mile

Head up through the trees, the stirring of the breeze and the scurrying of pheasants in the undergrowth the only sounds to break the silence. Follow the bridleway waymarks through the trees and eventually you reach a gate on the edge of the wood. The path swings left beneath power cables before

17

veering right at the bottom end of some ruined barns and byres. Follow a muddy path with the tree-shaded Ladhill Beck on your left and further on you reach a footbridge. Cross the bridge and then step over some stones to the opposite bank. Keep the fence on the left and follow the sunken path as it veers left. Go through a gate further up and climb gradually between fields until eventually you reach the road. Turn left and follow it south towards Hawnby.

This final leg of the walk demonstrates the timeless beauty and majestic scenery of the North York Moors. The views are matchless and in every direction there are soaring fells, lush green dales and sweeps of open moorland. Over to the left the bulk of Easterside Hill can be seen reaching skyward and to the right are the lower slopes of Hawnby Hill Crag. Pass Long Acres Farm on the left and continue down the lane back into the centre of Hawnby.

Rievaulx Abbey and Old Byland

Length of walk: 6 miles
Start/finish: Rievaulx Abbey, half a mile from the B1257, north west of Helmsley. Avoid using abbey car park at busy times
Terrain: Attractive woodland tracks, lanes and field paths as far as Old Byland. Beyond the village, the walk follows field paths and tracks to join a riverside path running along Ryedale's floor. Several gentle ascents and one climb through woodland

The remains of Rievaulx Abbey, one of the great monastic houses of the North of England, represent the jewel in Ryedale's crown. From here this delightful walk joins forces with the Cleveland Way, picking its way along Nettle Dale's gloriously verdant floor before heading north across open farmland to the village of Old Byland. The final lap hugs a stretch of the enchanting River Rye, cutting through pretty woodland and across lush meadows on its return to Rievaulx.

Follow the road through the hamlet of Rievaulx, keeping the abbey ruins on the left and the Rye on the right.

Rievaulx Abbey is one of the largest and most impressive Cistercian abbeys in England. Founded in 1131 by Walter l'Espec, Rievaulx once boasted 140 choir monks and 600 lay brothers. They led busy, industrious lives, tending 15,000 sheep, toiling in the fields and fishing the nearby river. It is easy to see why they chose Ryedale as a site of worship. Even today, Rievaulx's glorious, wooded valley setting generates an atmosphere that is conducive to quiet reflection and meditation.

There is a choice of routes at the next junction. To visit Helmsley, bear left and follow the Cleveland Way through woodland and across field enclosures. To continue the main walk, turn right and cross the graceful, three-arched bridge spanning the river. Pass Ashberry Farm, with its neat, whitewashed buildings, and a turning for Old Byland on the right, continuing ahead on the Cleveland Way towards Thirsk.

The lane runs past Hagg Hall before turning left. Keep going for about 100yds/m, then turn right onto a track, following the next stretch of the Cleveland Way through Nettle Dale. Pass through the gate and skirt some ponds on the right. Bear right at the next right-of-way sign, cross a shallow beck and go through a gate. Make for a stile and aim for woodland on the far side of the meadow. On reaching the trees, veer left and follow the path as it runs diagonally up the wooded hillside.

Pass a sign for Old Byland and approach a gate at the top of the wood. Follow the field boundary, with the buildings of Old Byland ahead. Go through two gates, continue straight on at a junction of tracks, where there are two gates on the right, and make for a gate and wall ahead. Cut through an area of woodland scrub, keeping left when the bridle path forks, and go diagonally up the grassy hillside to a gate leading out to the road.

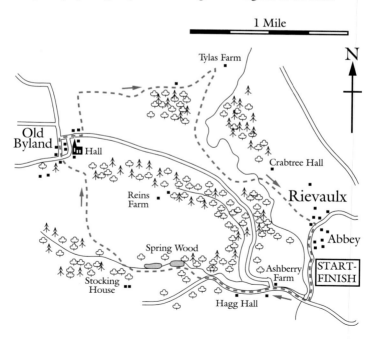

Turn right, passing the Old Byland sign and the outbuildings of Valley View Farm. Avoid a turning on the left and follow the road into the village, its wide main street overlooked by rows of stone houses and cottages. A red, pre-British Telecom telephone box can be seen here. Bear right at the top of the street, heading towards Helmsley and Rievaulx, and continue as far as a ladder-stile on the left, just beyond some extensive farm outbuildings either side of the road.

Cross two fields, keeping the boundary on the left, then bear right at the sign for Tylas. Follow the waymarked path over a number of enclosures before joining a track leading to Tylas Farm. Wooded Ryedale can be seen ahead now, with the remains of Rievaulx Abbey nestling amid the trees. Follow the track through a gate by Tylas Barn and continue down towards the farm.

Bear sharp right, about 75yds/m before the buildings, and follow the drive down the slope. Just before the next rise, cross a stile on the left and follow the grassy path along the dale floor, with the Rye close by on the left. Make for a stretch of boardwalk, with the river prettily enclosed by trees. Cross another stile and keep on the waymarked path to meet a track.

Turn left, cross the Rye and look for a footpath sign for Rievaulx after about 200 yards. Pass under the boughs of an oak tree and follow the waymarked path towards the abbey. Cross two stiles by the river and skirt several meadows, keeping alongside trees and a fence. Make for a kissing gate, with a dramatic view of Rievaulx ahead, set against a backdrop of trees. Pass through two more gates and head for the road. Turn right for Rievaulx Abbey.

Helmsley, Carlton and Ash Dale

> **Length of walk: 5 miles**
> **Start/finish: Helmsley Market Square**
> **Terrain: Firm road surfaces and farm tracks; stretches of sheltered path and track in Ash Dale**

Circular walk beginning in Helmsley and then heading for the peace and quiet of Ash Dale. After visiting the sleepy village of Carlton, the route follows a quiet lane back to town.

From the centre of Helmsley walk along the A170 towards Scarborough, eventually turning left at the sign for Carlton. Pass Helmsley Youth Hostel on the left and follow the road out of the town. When you reach a public footpath and a seat on the left, with a no right-of-way sign opposite, leave the road and follow the path through the trees and undergrowth. The path soon curves right and begins to head up through Ash Dale. The steeply rising slopes of the dale and its sheltered, wooded setting give this stretch of the walk adequate protection on a breezy day. The track can be very wet and muddy in places, particularly after heavy rain. Continue between carpets of bracken and through mixed woodland characterized by conifers and beech trees — among other species. You may be fortunate enough to spot roe deer in Ash Dale.

Progress through Ash Dale involves a gentle, steady climb through the trees and eventually the track dwindles to a narrow path. Pass through a dilapidated gate, with a waymark pointing ahead, and continue for some time until you come up to a junction with a track. Turn right (signposted Carlton) and follow Keld Lane through the trees. Emerge from the woodland, pass through a gate and follow the lane across breezy ground, cutting between grassy verges, fields and hedgerows. This stretch of the walk offers expansive views. Ahead are the trees of neighbouring Riccal Dale. Turn right at the road and walk into Carlton.

Pass the church on the left and walk down the lane through the village. Keep on the road as it heads south out of Carlton, heading towards Helmsley. The walk cuts through a landscape of rolling fields and hedgerows and beside the road are rows of trees — oak and beech among them. Pass a barn and some stone outbuildings, followed by the entrance to Cliff Stud. At this point the road begins to descend towards Helmsley, the buildings of the town clearly seen below. Head for the A170, turn right and return to the Market Square in the centre of Helmsley.

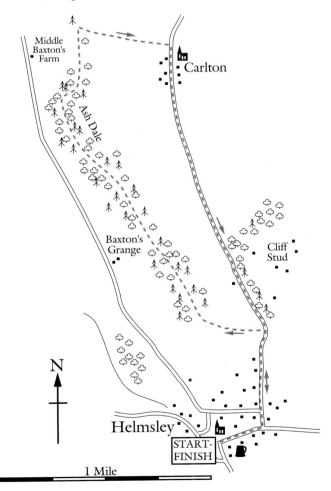

Helmsley and the River Rye

Length of the walk: 2¹/₂ miles
Start/finish: Helmsley Market Square
Terrain: Mainly level paths and tracks; there are muddy stretches and some sections can be rather overgrown in summer

Rectangular walk starting in Helmsley town centre and following a stretch of the Ebor Way beside the River Rye.

Begin the walk in Helmsley's spacious Market Square, overlooked by sturdy stone cottages, picturesque inns and hotels. In the corner lies an ancient market cross and dominating the scene is the imposing Gothic statue of William, 2nd Earl of Feversham. Duncombe Park, family home of the Earls of Feversham, lies about one mile to the south-west of the town. The original mansion was destroyed by fire towards the end of the 19th century and the Fevershams invested a great deal of money in rebuilding it. For many years it was leased as a prep school for girls. Nearby, too, and well worth a look, is the ruined Norman keep of Helmsley Castle, surrounded by spectacular earthworks. During the Civil War, the castle, which is now in the care of English Heritage, surrendered to Parliamentary forces after a three-month siege in 1644 following the Battle of Marston Moor.

Leave Helmsley by taking the A170 road towards Thirsk. Turn left into Ryegate immediately before the bridge spanning the River Rye and follow the road between rows of stone cottages. Compared with Helmsley's Market Square and surrounding streets, this residential corner of the town is quiet and largely undiscovered. Turn right after a short distance into Sawmill Lane, the walk now coinciding with the route of the Ebor Way, a 70-mile walk which links Helmsley with the West Yorkshire town of Ilkley. This long-distance trail takes its name from Eboracum — Roman York.

Follow the lane over some speed humps and alongside bungalows and offices. Keep going when the lane becomes a stony track and follow it round to the right. There is a signpost here for the Ebor Way. Avoid a turning on the left and veer right, then left at further Ebor Way signs. Go through a gate and follow the track across a tree-ringed field, the routine sounds of Helmsley fading now as you delve ever further into the countryside. On reaching the entrance to Helmsley Waste Water Treatment Works, cross a stile and follow the Ebor Way alongside the picturesque Rye. The river is the haunt of dippers and grey wagtails — among other species of bird. You may even be lucky enough to glimpse a kingfisher in this part of Ryedale.

Continue on the riverside path and skirt several fields. Look for a river crossing just beyond a stile; disregard it and branch off to the left. The river sweeps round in a wide curve to meet you on the far side of the field. Keep to the riverside path as it crosses rough ground and meadows. As you approach a stand of trees, begin to curve away from the river towards a gate and stile. Make for a second gate leading into an enclosure, turn left and make for a galvanized gate beyond which are the remains of a long

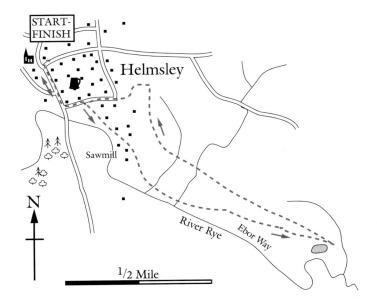

abandoned railway which originally linked Helmsley with York and Scarborough. Pass under the stone bridge and turn immediately left. Go through a gate and follow the grassy path through open countryside. Immediately beyond the large field on the right, veer diagonally right across farmland to the line of a hedge. Keep it on the left and walk along to a gate.

Go straight on to a second gate and join a track. On reaching a footpath, turn right and follow it beside the Spittle Beck. Avoid a stile on the right and cross a footbridge over the beck just before reaching the road. Turn left for several steps, heading straight on when the road bends left. Follow the path through light woodland and the remains of Helmsley railway station platform can be identified among the trees and vegetation. The site is being developed as a nature reserve by Helmsley Wildlife Watch Group. Follow the path round to the right, cutting between a fence and stone wall. The old station building and yard can be seen on the left now and ahead of you is the splendid outline of Helmsley Castle, standing out proudly against the skyline. Go straight on at the road, following it into Ryegate. Turn right on reaching the A170 and return to Helmsley town centre.

Harome and the River Riccal

Length of walk: 2³/₄ miles
Start/finish: Harome, 2 miles south-east of Helmsley
Terrain: Easy road walking and field paths, wet in places; no steep climbs

Easy rectangular walk exploring the gentle countryside around the village of Harome. The final leg of the walk follows the River Riccal.

The village of Harome includes a number of handsome Regency and Georgian houses, as well as some picturesque, thatched cottages. The village's ancient cruck timber-framed manor house was dismantled and rebuilt at the Ryedale Folk Museum in Hutton-le-Hole, near Kirkbymoorside. From the parish church of St Saviour in the centre of Harome, follow the road north through the village, heading towards Helmsley. On the left is The Star Inn, a famous pub/restaurant in the area, originally a 14th-century longhouse built as a hostelry for travelling monks. The gardens include a large ash.

Veer right at the fork for Pockley and you cannot fail to spot the large sycamore tree dominating the junction. Pass Sycamore Terrace on the right and follow the single-track lane out of the village. Harome's cricket ground soon looms into view on the right. The road cuts through a gentle lowland landscape and further on a conveniently placed seat can be seen in the right-hand verge, ideal for pausing to rest and admire the pastoral scene. The seat, located beneath the boughs of an overhanging oak tree, offers cooling shade on a warm summer's day.

Disregard a track running off to the left and keep to the lane. When it eventually bends left, at a sign for Harome, Hovingham, Pockley and Helmsley, turn right by Harome Heads Farm and follow the tarmacked lane beneath overhanging trees. Pass a hedge and some wooden panel fencing which encloses Shaw Moor Farm and then turn immediately right to follow a path. Negotiate a stile before heading across a field, passing beneath power cables. Keep the hedgerow on the left and make for the field corner where there is another stile. Skirt the next field by turning right and following the boundary.

Bear left in the corner and continue for almost 100 yards until you spot a gap in the scrub and undergrowth. Follow the path through long grass and between bushes and shortly you reach a stile on the edge of a field. Keep ahead to the corner and cross the next stile followed by a footbridge. Maintain the same direction in the next field, cross several more stiles and emerge at the road on the eastern outskirts of Harome. Go forward to the junction with the village street, turn right and then immediately left. Follow the road round the right-hand bend to reach Harome Methodist Chapel, built in memory of various local residents whose names are inscribed on the walls of the building.

Cross a stile opposite the chapel and head out across this elongated field to a stile in the far boundary. Continue ahead in the next field, making for a line of trees in the bottom boundary. Look for a stile and cross the River Riccal via the footbridge. Turn right and make for a stile in the field corner. The meandering river is prettily enclosed by trees on this charming stretch of the walk, their boughs reaching down to the water's edge. Keep following the riverside path until you reach a stile leading out to the road. Over to the left are the outbuildings of Aby Green Farm.

Turn right and then keep left at the fork. The sound of rushing water soon becomes audible as you approach Harome Mill. On the right is Rose Cottage, a charming little dwelling surrounded by thatched cottages and more modern development. Pass the village duck pond, with its feathered inhabitants often seen meandering about in the road. Follow the road round to the right and return to the centre of Harome. If you are in need of rest and refreshment after the walk, the Pheasant Inn, once the village blacksmith's workshop, is handily located on the right as you approach the junction.

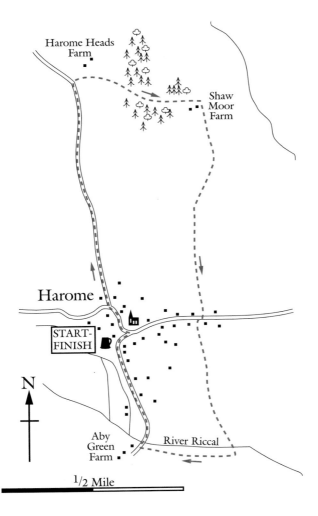

Harome Heads Farm

Shaw Moor Farm

Harome

START-FINISH

N

Aby Green Farm

River Riccal

1/2 Mile

Nunnington and the River Rye

Length of walk: 5 miles
Start/finish: Nunnington village, south of the A170 between Helmsley and Kirkbymoorside
Terrain: A breezy walk using good, clear tracks, green lanes and a very pleasant riverside path

This fine walk explores spacious rural landscapes on the southern edge of the North York Moors, the wide horizons and distant vistas suggesting a regal, expansive land of agricultural estates and occasional villages. This corner of Ryedale doesn't feature that prominently on the tourist map. There are glimpses of the national park here and there, but on the whole the walk and its surroundings seem far removed from the character of the North York Moors.

Nunnington Hall, a mellow 17th-century manor house in the care of the National Trust, includes a splendid oak-panelled hall and a remarkable Carlisle collection of miniature rooms, fully furnished to reflect different periods. A stroll in the grounds reveals a walled garden where ducks and peacocks strut about on the bank of the River Rye. Nunnington Hall, which is open to the public during the summer months, has been a family home for more than 400 years.

From the northern entrance to Nunnington Hall, follow the road south over the River Rye, then bear immediately right and walk through the village. Pass Nunnington Studios and follow the lane round to the left and up the hill, passing the Royal Oak on the right before reaching the junction by the church of All Saints and St James.

The porch contains a charming pencil sketch of the church by a small boy who was evacuated to Nunnington during the early years of the Second World War. Frederick Millington records his impressions and memories of that uncertain

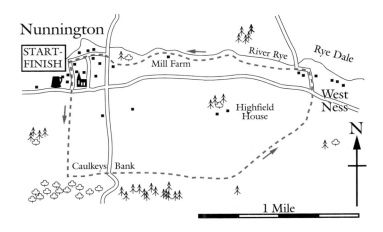

time, and why being a 'vaccy' in Nunnington, while storm clouds gathered over the country, as well as the rest of the world, was so precious to him.

Cross the road and join a public bridleway running south between hedges and banks of cow parsley. Clusters of wild, bright, red poppies can sometimes be seen on this stretch of the walk, which, even here, in the peace and quiet of the countryside, can quickly evoke disturbing images of war, bloodshed and brutality. Follow the track with glimpses of distant fields and woodland. The villages of Oswaldkirk and Ampleforth, straddling the southern boundary of the North York Moors National Park, lie away to the west.

Reach a conveniently placed seat on the right. From here much of Ryedale can be seen; to the north the heather moors rise gently to the horizon. Follow the straight track to a junction, turn left and, with Caulkleys Wood on the right, head for the road at Caulkleys Bank. Nearly 2 miles/3.2km to the south lies the pretty village of Hovingham, nestling against the backdrop of the Howardian Hills. Hovingham Hall was built about 1760 by Thomas Worsley, one of whose descendants is the Duchess of Kent.

Cross the road by a seat 'in memory of Clement and Eva Powell of York, who frequently enjoyed the view from here'. Continue on the next stretch of public bridleway, past a stone-built Ordnance Survey trig pillar on the left. These markers, superseded by advanced satellite technology, were originally used to record an exact height established by surveying instruments. On reaching a junction of tracks, bear left, then veer half right after a few steps and continue on the bridleway, following the grassy track between hedgerows.

Pass some barns on the right and descend gently to the junction at West Ness. Turn left and follow the road to the right (signposted Welburn and Kirkbymoorside). Head round the left-hand bend, passing some farm outbuildings at West Ness Hall, and approach Ness Bridge, beneath which flows the River Rye, its water plants streaming just below the surface.

Turn left immediately before the bridge and join a footpath running alongside the river. Cross a stile and skirt a field with the Rye on the right. Pass through a gate in the corner and continue to maintain the same direction. When the river makes a wide loop, keep ahead across the field, walk beside a row of trees and cross a dirt track. Aim slightly right to a stile in the field corner and continue ahead with the river still on the right, partly obscured by trees and foliage.

Pass through an opening in the field corner and head towards the buildings of Mill Farm. Cross two stiles with a gate in between them, keeping to the right of the farmhouse. On approaching the next boundary fence, make for a stile at the right-hand end of it, with a seat, overlooking a weir, just a few steps away.

Cross the field and make for a wooden gate adjacent to the ornamental gates of Nunnington Hall. Pass into the next field and keep the wall on the right. After a few moments the house looms into view. Follow the grassy bank, with the wall down below, pass a double-fronted stone-built house on the right and make for the next stile. Bear left to join the drive, following it to the road. Turn right and return to the village.
